DISCARD

HALLOWEEN FUN FOR EVERYONE

HALLOWEEN FUN FOR EVERYONE

Ferida Wolff & Dolores Kozielski

ILLUSTRATED BY JUDY LANFREDI

A Beech Tree Paperback Book
New York

Library of Congress Cataloging in Publication Data
Wolff, Ferida, 1946–
Halloween fun for everyone / by Ferida Wolff & Dolores Kozielski ;
illustrated by Judy Lanfredi.
p. cm.
Summary: Provides instructions for making costumes, decorating,
fixing fun foods, and playing games for a Halloween celebration.
1. Halloween—Juvenile literature. 2. Costume—Juvenile literature. 3. Halloween cookery—Juvenile literature. [1. Halloween.
2. Costume. 3. Halloween cookery.] I. Kozielski, Dolores. II.
Lanfredi, Judy, ill. III. Title.
GT4965.W65 1997 394.2646—dc21 97-7388 CIP AC

ISBN 0-688-15257-0
First Edition
10 9 8 7 6 5 4 3 2 1

For Paulette Kaufmann
—F.W.

For Barrie Van Dyke, with thanks
—D.K.

For Katie and Kelly Horton
—J.L.

CONTENTS

HALLOWEEN FUN FOR EVERYONE

THE SPIRIT OF HALLOWE'EN

What happens on Halloween? Suddenly, perfectly ordinary people put on crazy clothes, wild wigs, and outrageous makeup. They turn into magical creatures, fearsome animals, or the most unusual characters that ever came to town. Why do they do it?

Back 2,000 years ago, when the Druids lived, it wasn't unusual to dress up.

The Druids were Celtic people who were priests and poets, teachers and judges. They resided first in Gaul, in what is now western Europe, then migrated to England, Scotland, and Ireland. They taught that everyone had a soul that lived on after death.

The common people believed that on All Hallow Even, or Hallowe'en, the spirits came back to haunt them. To fool the spirits, they dressed up in white robes and horse-head masks. They lit huge bonfires and rang bells to scare the spirits away.

Begging for food in return for good wishes was a Celtic custom. The treat of a small cake was exchanged for a prayer for the soul of a dead relative. This practice was later brought to the United States from Ireland with something new added—tricks. This became our holiday of Halloween.

Today, many people still celebrate Halloween. They go out wearing costumes, ring doorbells, and yell, "Trick-or-treat!" But some people prefer to have an at-home celebration and have the spirit of Halloween last a lot longer.

At home you can create and play your own games, dress up your house as well as yourself, and make the strangest, tastiest food this side of the moon. This book shows you how to do all of it and more with a really *big* Haunted House Carnival!

Tricks from Halloweens past were all in fun, but in recent years some tricks have been harmful. If you decide to go out trick-or-treating, inspect the candy before eating it. Once in a while, someone will put a "trick" in the candy that could cause injury or illness. Throw away any treats that:

- have loose or tampered-with wrappings;
- are homemade or unwrapped, unless they come from a friend or relative;
- have foreign objects in them.

WEIRD WARDROBE

WITCH costume do you want to wear? How about an ancient mummy or a sea monster? Here are costumes for everyone and a special section of Flip-Flop costumes (see page 22) that shows you how, with very little effort, to change one costume to its opposite. Lots of weird and wacky characters can be your friends on Halloween night.

MAKEUP!

Makeup can wake up your costume. But some people have allergic reactions to makeup, so test it first. Three days before you want to wear it, rub a small amount on the inside of your wrist. Leave it on for two or three hours. If you notice itching, stinging, burning, or a rash, don't use it. Commercial makeup kits should have an FDA seal of approval. Hypoallergenic makeup is less likely to irritate your skin. You can remove most makeup with cold cream or baby oil, or you can follow the kit's instructions for removal. Then wash your skin thoroughly with soap and water.

Ancient Mummy

Halloween's here, so don't drag your feet. This is an easy *costomb* to make. You can become ancient in no time at all.

THIS IS WHAT YOU NEED:

- white turtleneck and pants
- white sneakers
- hollow-mesh polishing cloth, 6-ounce size (found in automotive stores)
- friend or parent
- scissors
- ruler
- twine
- wide masking tape
- white creme eye shadow
- gray eye shadow

THIS IS WHAT YOU DO:

1. Put on the turtleneck, pants, and sneakers.
2. Unfold the polishing cloth. Open one end of the cloth. It should form a long tube. Step inside the tube feet first and pull it up over your body.

3. Have your friend or parent pull the tube over your head and tape any excess from the top to the back of your head.

4. Have your friend pinch the cloth away from your face and carefully snip a hole for your face to fit through. Spread the opening to fit your face, but keep your ears covered.

5. Have your friend or parent measure 2 inches down from each shoulder, pull the cloth away from your body, and then carefully snip a small opening with the scissors. Push your arms through.

6. Cut several lengths of twine, 6 to 12 inches. Unravel and shred the ends. Stick the twine to pieces of tape.

EEEK!

7. Tape the polishing cloth to shape a neck with taped twine.

8. Stick remaining tape and twine here and there to create a ragged look.

9. Rub the white eye shadow over your face. Rub a ring of gray eye shadow around each eye.

It took a long time to make a mummy—seventy days! First the body's organs were removed. Then the body was dried out in a salt compound and preserved with resins and oils. Finally it was wrapped in linen for all time.

14

Fortune-Teller

What can you see in the Silver Circle? Reflections of all who cross your path. The future is in the cards—if you know how to read them!

THIS IS WHAT YOU NEED:

- hole punch
- 10 playing cards
- long skirt, or make Witch's skirt (on page 23) in bright fabric
- needle and thread
- clear round plastic lid
- white craft glue
- silver glitter
- 27 inches of ribbon
- plain T-shirt
- 30-inch square scarf

THIS IS WHAT YOU DO:

1. Punch a hole in the center top of each card. Scatter the cards face up on the front of the skirt.

2. Thread the needle. Make a knot at one thread end. Push the needle up from the inside of the skirt through the hole in one card, over the top, and back into the skirt, making a loop. Pull the thread tight. Make 3 or 4 more loops, and then tie off the thread inside. Repeat with all the cards.

3. Punch 2 holes, 1 inch apart, near one edge of the plastic lid. Spread the glue evenly on the lid's indented side. Sprinkle on glitter. Let dry. Thread the ribbon through the holes. Make a necklace by knotting the ribbon ends together.

4. Put on the T-shirt and skirt. Wear the Silver Circle necklace.

5. Fold the scarf into a triangle. Drape the triangle on your head, point in back, with the front overlapping your forehead. Tie the loose ends in back of your head. Make a double knot.

Cards were invented in China more than 1,000 years ago. They were used for predicting the future long before playing cards were introduced for entertainment.

Wild Wig

This wig is for boys and curls alike. Make it in your hair color, any hair color, or many hair colors—it's guaranteed to tease a smile from your friends.

THIS IS WHAT YOU NEED:

- 1 skein of yarn, any color
- 1 pipe cleaner, to match the yarn
- ruler or tape measure
- scissors
- bobby pins

THIS IS WHAT YOU DO:

1. Make the pipe cleaner into a circle and twist the ends together.
2. Measure and cut off a 24-inch strand of yarn. Cut at least 75 more. Cut more for a fuller wig.
3. Fold a strand in half. With your fingers, make a loop at the fold and hold it to the circle. Bring the loose ends up through the loop and tighten to the circle. Continue looping the yarn all around the circle to make a full wig. Spread the strands evenly.

4. Put the circle on top of your head. Pull some of your hair up through the circle and blend with the yarn. Fasten in place with bobby pins.
5. If you want bangs, pull some of the strands in front of your face and cut them eyebrow length. Be careful not to cut your own hair.

Wigs have been made of wool, fur, horsehair, wire, nylon, human hair, and straw. Some of the reasons wigs are worn are: to protect the person's own hair; as a disguise; for religious reasons; and for fashion and beauty.

Cleopatra

Barge into the room like an Egyptian queen. A headdress, a necklace, and a simple cloth transform you into royalty, as regal as the gold you wear.

THIS IS WHAT YOU NEED:

- 16 sparkly gold 12-inch pipe cleaners
- aluminum foil
- ruler or tape measure
- scissors
- black Wild Wig (on page 16)
- turtleneck and matching leggings
- sandals
- hollow-mesh polishing cloth, 6-ounce size (found in automotive stores)
- black eyeliner pencil
- red lipstick

THIS IS WHAT YOU DO:

1. For the headdress, make a 24-inch long pipe cleaner by twisting 2 together end to end. Repeat 4 more times. Place two of them side by side. Bend them around your head and twist the ends closed sideways. Put the remaining 3 long pipe cleaners aside.

2. Cut an 8- x 6-inch strip of foil. With the shiny side out, loosely roll up the 8-inch side into a snake shape. With your thumb, press flat 2 inches at one end for the cobra's head. Roll the remaining 6 inches tighter. Attach the snake to the headdress by coiling onto the pipe-cleaner circle. Shape the snake into an S with the head facing out.

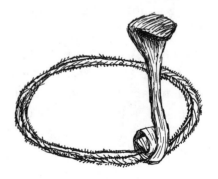

3. Make a black Wild Wig.

4. To form a necklace, make a U with one of the long pipe cleaners from Step 1. Measure 2 inches from each end and twist the ends of another long pipe cleaner onto the first. Measure 1 inch from the second long pipe cleaner and twist onto the third long pipe cleaner.

5. Take a 12-inch pipe cleaner and fold it in half. Hang the fold in the center of the upper U. Twist the pipe cleaner once over the upper U. Continue twisting. Twist over the middle U. Continue twisting over the bottom U. Form a circle with the remaining length of the pipe cleaner and twist ends closed sideways.

6. To make Cleopatra's belt, twist the ends of the remaining pipe cleaners together into one long strand.

7. Put on the turtleneck, leggings, and sandals. Step into the polishing-cloth tube. Drape a part over one shoulder and let the other part hang. Twist the belt around your waist, letting the ends hang down. Adjust the cloth to be skirt-like.

8. Outline your eyes, top and bottom, with the eyeliner pencil. On the edge of each eye, going toward your ear, draw a thick line. Put on deep red lipstick.

9. Put on the necklace and twist the ends closed behind your neck. Put on the Wild Wig. Place the headdress on top of the wig.

The snake on the ancient crowns of Egyptian kings and queens was a cobra. Its eyes were thought to be the burning eyes of a god who shot flames to protect the wearer from enemies.

Sea Monster

Here is a sea-green creature covered with kelp and dripping with seaweed—well, almost. This is an easy, no-sew costume to make at the last minute.

THIS IS WHAT YOU NEED:

- green plastic trash bag without handles
- scissors
- ruler or tape measure
- 2 pipe cleaners to match your hair color
- twine
- green or gray turtleneck and sweatpants
- blue or green creme eye shadow
- silver glitter

THIS IS WHAT YOU DO:

1. Cut off a 1-inch strip around the opening of the trash bag. Set the strip aside. Cut a hole in the center of the bottom seam of the bag, big enough to fit over your head.

19

2. Measure 6 inches down from one bottom corner of the bag. Then cut a 1-inch square for an armhole. Repeat on the other side.

3. From the bottom opening, cut several slits halfway up, varying them 2 to 5 inches apart.

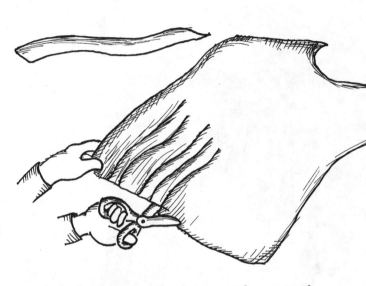

4. Twist the pipe cleaners together to make a circle that fits your head. Cut 10 lengths of twine, 12 to 24 inches long. Tie one end of each around the circle. Unravel the twine to make it stringy.

5. Cut the plastic strip that you set aside into 3 or 4 pieces of different lengths. Tie one end of each onto the circle between the twine to finish the headdress.

6. Put on the turtleneck and sweatpants. Pull the trash bag down over your head and push your arms through the armhole squares. CAUTION—DO NOT KEEP THIS OR ANY OTHER PLASTIC BAG ON YOUR FACE.

7. Tie twine around your waist. Cut more lengths of twine, tie them to the waistband, and let them dangle. Unravel the twine ends.

8. Cover your face with the eye shadow. Dab on a little glitter with your fingertips.

9. Put on the headdress, being careful not to obstruct your vision.

Q. Why wouldn't the sea monster weigh himself?

A. Because he didn't want to step on his scale.

Cave Dweller

Come on, don't cave in to pressure to buy a costume—make your own. You won't have to be hit over the head to figure out how to make this one, it's so easy.

THIS IS WHAT YOU NEED:

- 1 yard of fake-fur material
- scissors
- pair of worn-out or too short pants
- turtleneck
- twine (optional)
- gray powdered eye shadow
- 1 cotton swab

THIS IS WHAT YOU DO:

1. Fold the fur in half widthwise. In the middle of the fold, cut an opening big enough to put your head through.

2. Cut zigzags on the bottom of the fur and the pants legs.

3. Put on the turtleneck and pants. Put the fur over your clothes. Tie a length of twine around your waist.

4. Brush the eye shadow over your face and forehead. Wet the cotton swab and draw wrinkly lines through the powder. Run your fingers through your hair and really mess it up!

5. Extras will add to your costume but aren't necessary: hairy bedroom slippers, or a cleaned and dried chicken bone tied to a string around your neck. Or make a very hairy Wild Wig (page 16).

Cro-Magnon (pronounced crow mag-nen) *was an early form of human who lived in caves and used stone and bone tools.*

Flip-Flop Costumes

These costumes keep you guessing. Choose the first costume or flip-flop to its opposite with a few simple changes. The Witch can become a Warlock, and the Sheriff becomes a Cattle Rustler. Or you and a friend make both and go as a pair of opposites.

Witch

Witch costumes are a familiar sight on Halloween, but look again—there's something different about this one: The cape is the skirt, and the skirt is the cape. Add a Wild Wig, a pointy hat, and a broom, and you'll sweep everyone off their feet.

THIS IS WHAT YOU NEED:

- scissors
- ruler or tape measure
- black, loose-weave, 54-inch-wide cotton fabric—2 yards for Witch, 1 yard for Warlock
- 4 yards of black yarn
- needle with large eye
- Wild Wig (on page 16)
- dark turtleneck and pants or leggings
- friend
- Molefoam (found in foot-care displays)
- green creme eye shadow
- eyebrow pencil
- broom
- pointy hat

ADDITIONAL MATERIALS FOR THE WARLOCK:

- newspapers
- 1 tube of fluorescent material paint
- pencil
- large paper grocery bag
- stapler and staples
- purple creme eye shadow
- large branch

THIS IS WHAT YOU DO:

1. Cut the fabric into 2 pieces, 1 yard x 54 inches each. Cut the yarn into 2 pieces, each 2 yards long.
2. Thread one length of yarn through the needle. Baste the 54-inch side of one piece of fabric, 1½ inches from the top edge. (See next page.)
3. Push the fabric toward the center from both ends, leaving about 6 inches of yarn on each side for tying the cape around your neck. Make thick knots on the ends of the yarn.
4. Repeat Step 2 with the other yarn and fabric to make the skirt. Knot the yarn ends. Adjust to fit your waist.

5. Make a Wild Wig.
6. Put on the turtleneck and pants or leggings. Wrap the skirt around your waist and tie. If the skirt falls below your ankles, have your friend cut off the extra fabric.
7. To make a wart, cut a small circle from the Molefoam. Pull a few fuzzies off the wig. Remove the backing of the Molefoam,

press the hairy fuzz to the stickum, and then press the Molefoam to your chin.

8. Cover your face, wart, and hands with the green eye shadow. Draw wrinkle lines by your mouth, eyes, and on your forehead and a dot on the wart with the eyebrow pencil.

9. Put on the Wild Wig and hat and carry a broom.

HOW TO BASTE

Push the threaded needle into the fabric through to the other side then out again ½-inch away from where you started. Repeat to make a straight line of loose stitches. A running stitch is done the same way except the stitch size is ¼-inch.

Long Basting Stitch

_ _ _ _ _

Running Stitch

_ _ _ _

The word hex comes from the German hexe, *meaning witch. A hex means an evil spell or curse.*

Warlock

Your friends will be spellbound when you turn a female witch into a male witch with the simple flip of a cape. The moon and the stars are yours to command, so use your magic and have fun decorating this Warlock costume.

THIS IS WHAT YOU DO:

1. Spread the newspapers on a flat surface. Spread out the fabric on the newspapers.

2. Draw crescent moons, stars, and lightning bolts on the fabric with the fluorescent paint. Let dry.

3. Repeat Steps 2 and 3 in the Witch's costume to make a cape.

4. To make the headdress, measure and mark 8 inches from the top of the grocery bag and cut off at mark. Discard the bottom. Cut open one of the seams. Trim off any notches. Turn the writing inside. Wrap the paper strip around your forehead to fit. Remove paper from your head, holding it in place. Hold ends together and have a friend staple them in place. Cut off the excess from the strip.

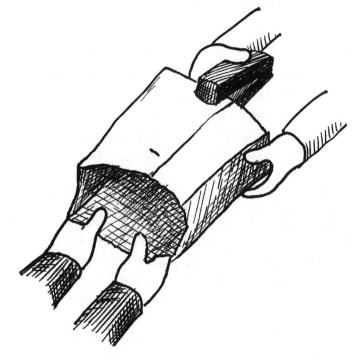

5. Put the headdress on your head. Have your friend carefully pencil arches over your eyebrows with a point between them and an arch around each ear. Remove the headdress and cut out the arches.

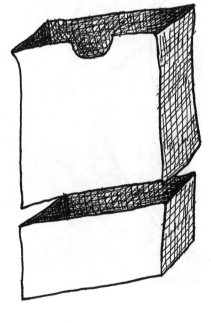

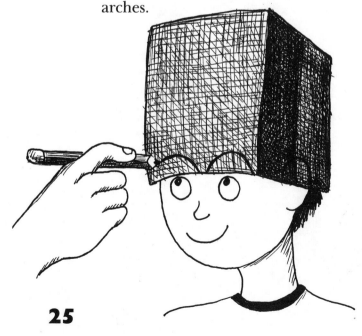

25

6. Paint the same designs around the headdress that you painted on the cape. Let dry.

7. Put on the turtleneck and pants.

8. Follow Step 8 of the Witch's costume, except use purple eye shadow and leave off the wart.

9. Tie on the cape. Put on the headdress. Carry the branch as a magic staff.

Warlock *is one of the many names given to a male witch.* Wizard, *sorcerer,* and oathbreaker *are some of the others.*

Sheriff

Jeans, checkered shirt, and bandanna are the keys to this costume, plus a set of "jail-house" keys. Leave your weapons at the door, pardner, 'cause you won't need them to have a blast.

THIS IS WHAT YOU NEED:

- pencil
- plain white paper
- cardboard
- paste or glue
- scissors
- heavy-duty aluminum foil
- marker
- double-sided transparent tape
- about 10 strands of yarn, 10 inches long, your hair color
- stiff hairbrush
- plaid or checkered shirt
- jeans
- belt
- boots or hightop sneakers
- bandanna
- assorted keys
- 1 pipe cleaner

ADDITIONAL MATERIALS FOR CATTLE RUSTLER:

- 4 pipe cleaners
- clothesline

Q. Why couldn't the sheriff keep the cattle rustler in jail?

A. Because he was an out-law.

THIS IS WHAT YOU DO:

1. Trace this 5-pointed star onto paper and paste it on the cardboard. Cut it out. Cover it with foil. From the cardboard scraps, cut a strip to fit across the star. Write SHERIFF on it with the marker. Place tape on back and stick it to the star.

2. Hold the yarn strands in one hand. Brush the yarn vigorously. Collect the fuzz that comes off in the brush, enough for 2 sideburns and 2 eyebrows. Put the fuzz on one side of each of 4 strips of tape. Place a strip of tape on each side of your face for fuzz sideburns. In the same way, stick on fuzz eyebrows above your own.

3. Put on the shirt, jeans, belt, and boots. Tie the bandanna around your neck. Tape the star to the shirt.

4. Thread the pipe cleaner through the "jailhouse" keys, the more the janglier. Make a pipe-cleaner ring around the belt or belt loop, and twist the ends together sideways.

Cattle Rustler

Flip the bandanna onto your face and flop over to the wrong side of town. The sheriff's star becomes your spur to steer clear of the law.

1. Trace 2 stars onto paper, paste them to cardboard, and cut them out. Cover them with foil. Carefully poke a hole with the scissors in the center of each star.

2. Make a long, 24-inch pipe cleaner by twisting 2 together end to end. Thread the pipe cleaners halfway through 1 star. Repeat with the remaining pipe cleaners and star to make spurs. Set aside.

3. Put on the shirt and jeans.

4. At your side, loop the clothesline several times over your belt.

5. Put on the boots. To attach your spurs, wrap the pipe cleaners around the boots at the ankle. Twist the ends together with the stars at the back.

6. Fold the bandanna into a triangle. Tie the bandanna behind your head, masking your nose and mouth.

Q. What did the outlaw say while he waited to hear if he would be strung up?

A. No noose is good noose.

EERIE EATING

Don't be fooled by what you find in this chapter. The food is familiar but put together in different and unusual ways. Halloween transforms common ketchup into a devilish hot sauce. Plain old grape juice becomes a knockout for vampires. And wait till you taste what happens to ho-hum hot dogs! You become the monster chef and have everyone eating out of your hands.

Wiggly Worm Sandwich

Fish aren't the only ones to get hooked on worms. These tummy ticklers are the best bait for hungry Halloween appetites.

THIS IS WHAT YOU NEED:

- 2 hot dogs for each sandwich
- cutting board
- knife
- pot
- water
- long-handled fork or tongs
- hamburger buns
- Devil's Salsa (see next recipe)
- spoon

THIS IS WHAT YOU DO:

1. Put a hot dog on the cutting board. Cut it into 4 long strips. Repeat with another hot dog.

2. Take each strip and make slits along one long edge, being careful not to cut it into pieces.

3. Put the cut strips into the pot. Cover them with cold water. Bring the water to a boil and cook the hot dogs for 5 minutes. They will curl into worms as they cook.

4. Turn off the heat. With the long-handled fork, carefully put 8 wiggly worms on a bun. Add 1 tablespoon of Devil's Salsa.

Ever hear the worm song?

Nobody likes me, everybody hates me,
I'm gonna eat some wor-r-rms.
Big fat juicy ones, little itty-bitty ones,
I'm gonna eat some wor-r-rms.
First you bite the head off, then you
suck the guts out, then you throw the
tail awa-a-ay.
Nobody knows how I can live on three
little worms a da-a-ay.

Devil's Salsa

Is this hot cold sauce or cold hot sauce?
The devil only knows—and you—when
you discover the fiery flavor of chili.

THIS IS WHAT YOU NEED:

- 1 bottle of ketchup, 14-ounce size
- 1½ teaspoons of onion powder
- 1 teaspoon of garlic powder
- 2 tablespoons of soy sauce
- 2 teaspoons of mustard
- 1 cup of water
- 1 teaspoon of Worcestershire sauce
- medium-size bowl
- 1 to 1½ tablespoons of chili powder
- knife
- cutting board
- 1 small tomato
- 1 small green pepper
- 1 small cucumber

THIS IS WHAT YOU DO:

1. Mix the first 7 ingredients together in
   the bowl. Add the chili powder: 1 tablespoon for mild; 1½ tablespoons for hot.

2. Finely chop the tomato, pepper, and
   cucumber. Add them to the bowl.

3. Refrigerate overnight. If the salsa is too
   thick, add water, 1 tablespoon at a time,
   until it's the thickness you like.

Q. Why did the devil get his shoes
   repaired?

A. He needed a new pair of souls.

Cauldron Cocoa

Brew up a cauldron of the best hot chocolate you've ever tasted. Pop in a pumpkin marshmallow, spice it up, and for a real twist, add a licorice-stick straw. You won't want to stop sipping until you're full.

THIS IS WHAT YOU NEED:

- large pot
- 1 gallon of milk
- 1 pound container of hot-cocoa mix
- ladle
- 16 hot cups, 9-ounce size
- ground cinnamon
- 16 pumpkin marshmallows
- knife
- 16 chocolate licorice twists

THIS IS WHAT YOU DO:

1. Pour the milk into the large pot, add the whole container of cocoa mix, and prepare according to package directions. Turn the heat on low.

2. For each serving, dip out one ladle of cocoa into a cup, sprinkle on a little cinnamon, and add a marshmallow.

3. Cut (or have the cocoa drinker bite) off each end of a licorice twist. Put it into the drink, to be used as a straw. Tell the drinker to sip carefully—the cocoa may still be hot!

Cinnamon was traditionally used by witches for purification in some of their rituals. It is still commonly used to ease the symptoms of colds, coughs, fevers, sore throats, and chills.

Hi ya, cutie!

Slimy Eyeballs

What's green, wiggles and jiggles, and really looks grape? You'll answer this riddle when you make this treat to *surpreyes* all your friends.

THIS IS WHAT YOU NEED:

- 1 cup water
- small saucepan
- pot holder
- heat proof bowl
- 3-ounce package of lemon-lime gelatin
- spoon
- 12 mini paper cupcake cups
- cupcake pan for 12 mini cupcakes
- tablespoon
- 12 purple seedless grapes
- 12 chocolate bits
- 6 graham crackers
- tray
- metal spatula or knife

THIS IS WHAT YOU DO:

1. Boil ½ cup of water in the saucepan. Using the pot holder, carefully pour the water into the bowl.

2. Add the gelatin to the bowl. Stir until dissolved. Add the other ½ cup of water. Stir again.

3. Put the cupcake cups into the cupcake pan. Add 3 tablespoons of gelatin to each cup. Put the pan into the freezer for 15 minutes.

4. Peel the skin off the grapes. Push 1 chocolate bit, point down, into the stem end of each grape.

5. Remove the gelatin from the freezer. Press 1 grape, chocolate end up, into the center of each cup to form eyeballs. Put the pan in the refrigerator until gelatin is set.

6. Break 6 graham crackers in half to make 12 squares. Put them on the tray.

7. Take the pan from the refrigerator just before serving. Remove 1 cupcake cup. Spread open the paper. Slide the spatula under the gelatin and slip the eyeball onto a graham-cracker square. Repeat with the other eyeballs.

Q. What happened when your cousin ate too many Halloween pies?

A. He turned into a plump-kin.

Witch's Upside-Down Trick-or-Treat Hats

These upside-down witch's hats are magically brimming with treats. The trick is to make the hats disappear along with the yummy things inside!

THIS IS WHAT YOU NEED:

- cardboard egg carton
- scissors
- waxed paper
- 3.5-ounce container of chocolate sprinkles
- water
- large frying pan
- small pot or saucepan
- 12-ounce bag of chocolate bits
- wooden spoon
- pot holder
- 12 sugar ice-cream cones
- 1 large bowl
- 1 cup of peanuts
- 8-ounce bag of pretzel nuggets
- 1 cup of raisins
- 1 cup of banana chips
- ½ cup of shelled pumpkin seeds

THIS IS WHAT YOU DO:

1. Turn the egg carton upside down. With the scissors, poke a hole through the circle of each egg section. Enlarge the hole with your finger. Set the egg carton aside.

2. Put a sheet of waxed paper on a flat surface. Pour a pile of sprinkles onto the paper.

3. Put ½ inch of water in the frying pan. Fill small pot with 1 cup of chocolate bits. Set the pot in the water and bring it to a boil. Turn off heat. Stir the bits with wooden spoon until melted.

4. Carefully take the pot out of the pan and place it in the sink where it won't burn the counter. Dip the rim of each cone into the melted chocolate. Swirl it around to coat about an inch. Then gently press the cone into the sprinkles to cover the chocolate—a scrumptious hat brim!

5. Place the point of the hat in one hole of the egg carton. Repeat with the other hats. Let the chocolate harden.

6. Mix the remaining ingredients in the bowl. Fill the hats with the mixture. There's enough for one refill for each hat.

It is said that wearing a brimmed hat backward brings seven miles of bad luck. And, if you wear a hat inside a house, you'll get a headache.

Knockout Vampire Punch

Is Dracula thirsting for your blood? Give him the one-two punch instead. First mix up this drink, then give it an extra kick with the sunny taste of vitamin C.

Yum! Delicious and Nutritious!

THIS IS WHAT YOU NEED:

- 6-ounce can of frozen orange juice concentrate
- 1 can of unsweetened pineapple juice, 46-ounces
- 2 cups of unsweetened grape juice
- large bowl
- 1-liter bottle of seltzer
- ladle
- cups

THIS IS WHAT YOU DO:

1. Mix the orange juice concentrate and the pineapple and grape juices in the bowl. Add the seltzer. Stir.
2. Ladle the punch into the cups. It makes 14 seven-ounce servings. For extra punch, add the Creepy Crawly Cubes (see next recipe).

Q. Why did the mechanical vampire fall from the belfry?

A. Because his bat-tery ran out of juice.

Creepy Crawly Cubes

Here are ice cubes crawling with flavor. They're made with orange juice instead of water—and just a little something more. Watch for a creepy surprise on the bottom of your drink when the cube disappears.

THIS IS WHAT YOU NEED:

- ice cube tray
- 1 cup orange juice
- assorted gummy worms or bugs

THIS IS WHAT YOU DO:

1. Fill the ice cube tray with the orange juice.
2. Add a worm or a bug to each cube.
3. Put the tray into the freezer until the cubes are solid.
4. Add one or more Creepy Crawly Cubes to your favorite drink.

IS AMERICA UNLUCKY?

The United States of America started as 13 colonies, which then became 13 states. The flag consisted of 13 stars and 13 stripes. The Great Seal of the United States has an eagle with one claw holding 13 arrows and the other, a branch with 13 leaves and 13 berries. The motto E Pluribus Unum (which means "one out of many") has 13 letters.

Ghost Soup

Warm up a chilly Halloween night with the haunting flavor of Ghost Soup. As you add the egg whites, a ghostly surprise appears in the pot.

THIS IS WHAT YOU NEED:

- knife
- 1 large apple
- 1 celery rib
- 1 small onion, peeled
- 1 medium carrot, peeled
- cutting board
- medium pot
- 3 cans of chicken broth, 14 ounces each
- ¼ cup of pumpkin, pureed or canned
- 2 teaspoons of dried basil
- 2 large egg whites
- fork
- small bowl
- ladle
- serving bowls

THIS IS WHAT YOU DO:

1. Peel the apple and remove the seeds. Finely chop the apple, celery, onion, and carrot.
2. Pour the chicken broth into the pot. Add the chopped apple and vegetables. Add the pumpkin and basil.
3. Simmer for 20 minutes on low heat.
4. Separate the whites from the yolks.

HOW TO SEPARATE EGGS

Tap the center of the eggshell against the rim of the bowl. Separate the shell halves with your thumbs. Tip the yolk back and forth between the shells, letting the egg white drip into the bowl.

5. Dip the fork into the whites, then drizzle the whites into the soup. Repeat until all the whites are used up.
6. Simmer for 5 minutes more. Ladle into bowls. This makes 8 servings, 6 ounces each.

DEVILISH DECORATING

A house doesn't look haunted without webs and bugs and mysterious shadows hanging around. Add pumpkins, a few hairy hands, and a spooky soundtrack for a convincing Halloween atmosphere.

Gobblin' Grab Greeting

It's mighty tempting to pull off a candy from this decorated pumpkin, but wait! You might want to play the Gobblin' Grab Game (page 59) with some of your friends first. You can always grab a treat later if there's anything left.

THIS IS WHAT YOU NEED:

- 1 egg white
- ½ teaspoon cream of tartar
- eggbeater
- mixing bowl
- 1 cup confectioners' sugar
- spoon
- 2 drops yellow food coloring
- 6 drops red food coloring
- 1 medium pumpkin
- assorted wrapped miniature candies, such as chocolate bars, kisses, and hard candies

THIS IS WHAT YOU DO:

1. Beat the egg white and the cream of tartar with the eggbeater until whites form stiff little peaks.

2. Add sugar, a little at a time. Beat well. Add the food coloring.

3. Wash and dry the pumpkin. Dab the bottoms of the wrapped candies into the sugar mixture and press them firmly onto the pumpkin. Let dry, about 2 hours.

4. You can use this as a centerpiece for the Eerie Eating Center (see page 76). When all the candy is off, don't forget to use the pumpkin—paint it, carve it, roast the seeds, or cook it into something wonderful.

IT'S ONLY A GOBLIN

If someone is knocking or creaking on stairs,
if the sofa is missing, and so are the chairs,
if the pots and pans clatter,
the dishes all shatter,
and no one can figure out
what is the matter,
don't worry or wonder or grumble or groan,
it's only a goblin—
so leave him alone!

Leaping Lint Bugs!

Yikes! Watch out—the lint bugs are leaping from the lintel above your door. They're not fleas, but visitors might want to flee from this surprising Halloween welcome.

THIS IS WHAT YOU NEED:

- dryer lint
- 3 plastic-bag ties, 3 more optional
- white glue
- 2 small plastic eyes
- scissors
- nylon elastic sewing thread
- ruler or tape measure
- transparent tape

THIS IS WHAT YOU DO:

1. Collect a small handful of dryer lint for each bug. Press the lint tightly.

2. Twist 1 tie once around the middle of the lint. Twist a tie between the middle and an end. Repeat with the other end. This forms 4 bug segments. Spread the tie ends to make 6 legs.

3. Glue the eyes onto 1 end segment. You may add wings by threading 2 more ties under the middle tie connecting the ends to make two wing shapes. Antennae are made by threading 1 end of a tie halfway through the tie by the head. Then roll down the antennae ends.

4. Cut a 30-inch length of elastic thread. Knot one end of the thread around the middle tie. Tape the other end to the inside frame above the front door. Make several lint bugs and vary their strings from 24 to 30 inches. Tape them in a row.

5. When someone comes calling, open the door all the way. The bugs will leap over it.

A lintel is the crossbeam over a door or window that holds the weight of the structure above it. Horseshoes are sometimes nailed over the lintel pointing up for good luck, pointing down to keep you safe.

43

Shadow Monster

Create your own monster with this special Halloween portrait. Don't worry about your drawing ability—this shadow monster is guaranteed to draw a laugh from even the grumpiest ghoul.

THIS IS WHAT YOU NEED:

- 6 large brown grocery bags
- scissors
- masking tape
- thumbtacks or tape
- lamp
- friend
- thick black marker
- 2 heavy cans
- crayons or colored markers (optional)

THIS IS WHAT YOU DO:

1. Cut down 1 side of a bag to the bottom. Cut off the bottom of the bag and discard. Repeat with the other 5 bags.

2. Place 1 bag, printed side up, open on the floor. Then tape another open bag to the first, short end to short end. Repeat with the third bag to form one long strip. Make a second strip with the remaining 3 bags. Now, tape the 2 strips together at the long sides to make one large brown paper sheet.

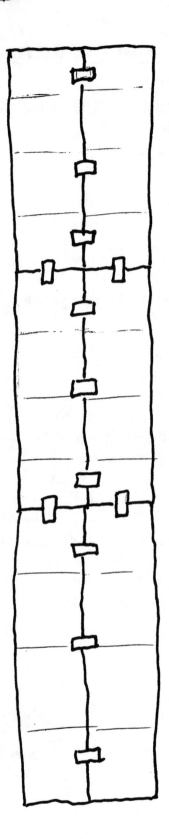

3. With the plain side facing out, thumb-tack or tape the paper widthwise to the top of the door frame only, covering the open doorway. The bags will trail on the floor.

4. Remove the shade from the lamp and place the lamp on the floor a few feet back from the printed side of the bags. Turn on the lamp, and turn off all other lights.

5. Have your friend stand between the bags and the lamp in a funny pose.

6. Take the marker and stand on the other side of the bags. You will see your friend's shadow. Pull the sheet of bags taut and anchor with the heavy cans.

7. Trace the outline of your friend on the bags. Switch places and have your outline drawn on the bags in a different pose. Add more arms and hands, if you wish.

8. Take down the shadow portrait. Cut away excess paper from the bottom. Color in the portrait with crayons or colored markers. You will have created a many-handed, two-headed monster.

9. Repeat Steps 1 through 8 for each Shadow Monster. Hang them in surprising places around the house.

The werewolf, a popular monster from traditional folklore, is a human who takes the form of an animal. In countries where wolves are not common, the human may become a bear or other animal form. Would that make it a werebear?

All Sorts o' Pumpkins

Not every pumpkin is meant to be carved. Try these other ways of decoration. Make a face or an animal or create your own work of art. Have your friends bring their own pumpkins—you supply the materials, they supply the talent.

THIS IS WHAT YOU NEED:

- newspaper
- head-size pumpkins
- toothpicks
- white glue
- knife
- scissors

Several of the following:

- cereal
- markers
- dried beans
- coffee filter
- yarn
- glitter
- colored electrical tape
- Molefoam
- pipe cleaners
- paper cups
- colored paper
- buttons
- marshmallows
- ribbon
- macaroni
- vegetables
- fruit
- orange peels
- licorice
- dried fruit
- sprinkles

THIS IS WHAT YOU DO:

1. Spread newspapers on your working surface. Put a pumpkin on top of the newspapers.

2. Make a food face using toothpicks and the white glue. Attach curved orange peels with toothpicks to the sides of the pumpkin for ears. Attach dried apple rings for eyes with grapes in the center. With the knife, cut curved sections from a green pepper and attach for eyebrows. Attach apple-skin lips and marshmallow teeth. Cut a mushroom in half and attach for a nose.

3. With the scissors, cut lengths of electrical tape to stick on for hair. Fasten on a coffee-filter hat with toothpicks.

4. Decorate a pumpkin, similar to the one described above, or be wildly creative with the other materials. Make tape stripes, licorice triangles, ribbon tails, macaroni, and button designs. Use Molefoam for anything—color it, shape it, and stick it right on. These pumpkins will brighten any pumpkin patch.

People have always felt the need to decorate things—clothing, houses, hats, skin, you name it. Buttons, for instance, were used only for decoration, not for fastening, until the 1300s.

Spooky Soundtrack

Scary noises turn an ordinary house into a haunted one. Record the creaks and squeaks that you usually ignore to make your personalized spooky soundtrack.

THIS IS WHAT YOU NEED:

- tape recorder
- blank 60-minute cassette

The sound of a hooting owl was feared by the Romans as being an ill omen. Many people still associate the owl's call with death or misfortune.

THIS IS WHAT YOU DO:

1. Put the blank cassette in the tape recorder. Be prepared to tape sounds that could be spooky when put together, such as a whistling teakettle, a howling dog, a telephone dial tone, jingling keys, a squeaky gate, thunder, an oven timer, or a knock on a wall.

2. Whenever you hear a sound you want to capture, turn on the tape, record, then immediately turn it off. Don't leave any gaps. Fill one side with sounds.

3. Play the tape as a scary background for your Halloween activities.

Wispy Webs

There are webs in the corners and webs on the chairs, wisps of webs all over the stairs. Actually, you can put these quick-to-make spooky webs anywhere you want them for a scare-raising experience.

THIS IS WHAT YOU NEED:

- 2-ounce package of rolled absorbent cotton (*not* cotton balls)
- transparent tape

THIS IS WHAT YOU DO:

1. Pull a piece of cotton off the roll.
2. Gently tease out the cotton, pulling on all sides, until it is very thin and webby. (To tease means to gently shred or pull apart, to separate the fibers and fluff them.) Make as few holes as possible.

3. Make lots of webs, and tape them in places that will surprise everyone. Tape webs to corners or walls or any place where they'll move in the breeze. Continue to tease the webs until you like their shapes.

4. The webs will change shape as their weight pulls them down. You can leave them alone—they'll still look spooky—or patch them with a small additional piece of teased cotton.

People have used cobwebs throughout the ages for healing cuts. They put the web onto the cut so it stopped the bleeding and acted as a delicate bandage.

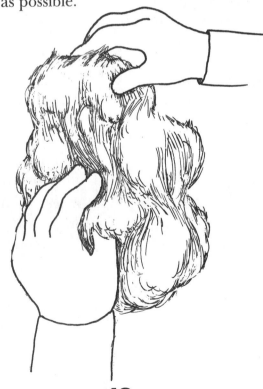

Hairy Scary Hands

Eeek! There's a hairy hand stuck in the door and another creeping out from back of the chair! It looks like there are werewolves on the loose just waiting to get their hands on you.

THIS IS WHAT YOU NEED:

- 1 package of disposable latex gloves
- 1 bag of cotton balls
- newspaper
- white glue
- glue brush
- dryer lint
- curved plastic nail tips
- purple nail polish

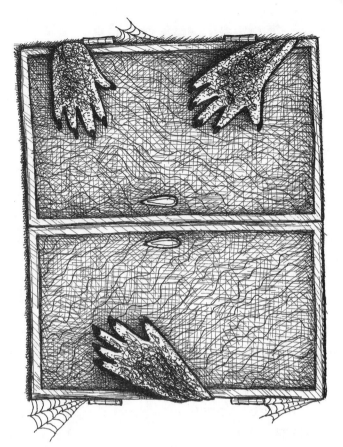

THIS IS WHAT YOU DO:

1. Stuff the fingers of 1 glove with cotton balls. Crumple 1 page of newspaper and stuff it into the palm.

2. Spread newspaper on a flat surface. Brush the glue on one side of the hand. Dab a blob of lint onto the glue. Let dry, then turn the hand over and do the other side.

3. On one side of the hand, glue the nails on the fingertips. Let dry. Polish the nails. Let dry.

4. Find a door that you won't be using, like a pantry or kitchen cabinet. Open the door and stuff the wrist of the hand between the door and the jamb by the door hinges. Be careful not to "jamb" your fingers in the door.

5. Make as many hands as you'd like and place them around the house—behind cushions, under chairs, coming out of a piano, behind the toilet—wherever you decide they'll have the creepiest effect.

An itchy right palm means money will be coming your way. When your left palm itches, though, you'll be giving money away.

49

Smell-o-pede

This decoration may not make sense to you when you start it, but when you put it all together, it becomes a "scent-sation." Clean socks are recommended, although those aged in the hamper will bring out the true personality of the Smell-o-pede.

THIS IS WHAT YOU NEED:

- scissors
- 2 foam cups, 7-ounce size
- 26 paper plates, 4 inches across, any color
- 2 pipe cleaners
- 10 pairs of dark socks
- 3 rectangular plastic laundry baskets
- double-sided tape

THIS IS WHAT YOU DO:

1. With the scissors, carefully poke 2 holes in the bottom of each cup and 2 in the center of each plate. Thread a pipe cleaner through both holes in 1 cup from the inside to the outside. Thread the pipe cleaner ends from the cup through the holes in a paper plate. Stuff a sock in the cup to form an eye. Repeat with the other cup, plate, and sock. Attach the eyes to the outside of one of the baskets' short ends by twisting the pipe cleaner around the mesh.

2. Turn the basket upside down. Push 2 inches of the tops of 3 socks, spacing them evenly, through the lowest mesh holes on each long basket side. Spread the socks out to make legs.

3. Repeat Step 2 with the other baskets.

4. Place the 3 baskets together in a row on the floor where people won't trip over them, to form a long Smell-o-pede.

5. For scales, cut or tear the remaining 24 plates in half. Starting on the top right of the Smell-o-pede, use the tape to make an overlapping row of 8 half-plates along each basket. Make a matching row along the left side.

Q. What centipede criminal mastermind always bugs Superman?

A. Legs Luthor

50

GHOULISH GAMES

Here's a collection of games you've never played before because you haven't created them yet. But don't worry, none of them takes very long to make. Dig up stuff around the house and change what's familiar into something that is unusual—and lots of fun for Halloween.

Family Plot Board Game

They're out on Halloween night! The ghosts leave the Family Plot to visit their old haunts. Can you get them back again? After a night on the town, they really need to Rest In Peace.

THIS IS WHAT YOU NEED:

- white poster board
- scissors
- game board following page 55
- photocopier
- transparent tape
- colored pencils—red, blue, green, and orange
- construction paper in red, blue, green, and orange
- ruler
- 2 plastic drinking straws
- rubber cement
- 2 dice

THIS IS WHAT YOU DO:

1. Cut the poster board to 17 x 11 inches.

2. Photocopy the game board on pages 56 and 57.

3. Cut along the outer lines of the copied pages. Glue or tape the two sections of the game to the poster board, joining them as indicated in the diagram on page 58.

4. Color the board as shown in the diagram.

5. Cut four ½-inch squares from each of the 4 sheets of construction paper. Cut each straw into 8 equal pieces. Glue one end of the each straw piece upright onto a colored square. These are the "ghost" playing pieces.

Tombstones placed flat on the earth were once thought to keep the dead from rising from the grave and haunting the living.

FAMILY PLOT

OBJECT OF THE GAME:

For 2 to 4 players

The players try to return their ghosts to the RIP section of the family plot by the end of Halloween Night.

RULES:

1. Players choose 4 ghosts of one color and a matching color tomb. Place one ghost in each of the four left-hand plots.

2. Each player throws the dice. The one with the highest number goes first. Play continues to the left.

3. To get out of each FAMILY PLOT, an odd number must be thrown. One ghost may move the full number thrown or 2 ghosts may move, 1 for each die. If a double is thrown, the player gets another throw. Only 2 turns are allowed on a double.

4. If a ghost lands on an occupied space, it sends the opponent's ghost back to an unoccupied plot on the left side of that ghost's family tomb.

5. Players must follow the instructions printed on any space where a ghost lands. Landing on an RIP space sends the ghost directly to RIP in its tomb, where the ghost is safe to rest in peace.

6. If the ghost lands on the ANCESTOR TREE, all the player's ghosts must be brought to that space from wherever they are on the board except the RIP space in the tomb. If an opponent then lands on the tree, it sends all of the first player's ghosts still on the space back to the family plot.

7. If a ghost lands on a space of its own color, it's safe from its opponents' ghosts and cannot be sent back to its plot.

8. An exact number must be thrown to get into the RIP space in the tomb. If a ghost is still outside the family plot and a number is thrown that is too high to allow it to enter RIP and no other family ghost can move, it must continue moving around the board. When all the ghosts have entered the family plot, only 1 die is used. If all of a player's ghosts are inside the family plot and the player rolls a number that is too high for them to move, then the player loses a turn.

9. Play continues around the board until one player gets all 4 ghosts back in RIP to win.

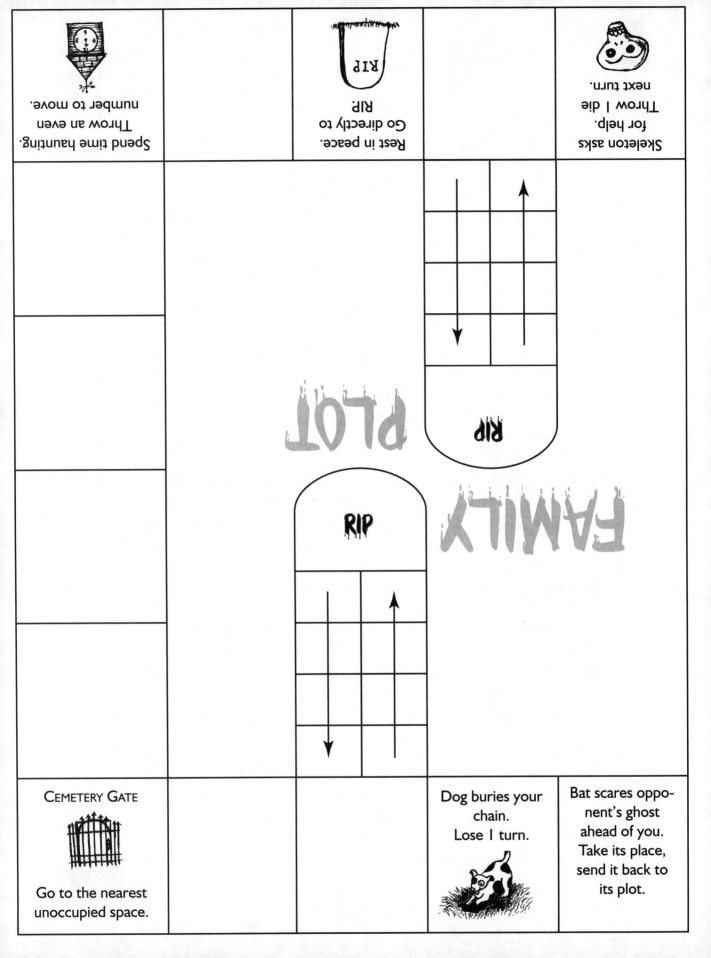

Spend time haunting.
Throw an even
number to move.

Rest in peace.
Go directly to
RIP

Skeleton asks
for help.
Throw 1 die
next turn.

RIP

RIP

PLOT

FAMILY

CEMETERY GATE

Go to the nearest
unoccupied space.

Dog buries your
chain.
Lose 1 turn.

Bat scares oppo-
nent's ghost
ahead of you.
Take its place,
send it back to
its plot.

Clouds cover the moon. Throw a double to move.

Black cat crosses your path. Take another turn.

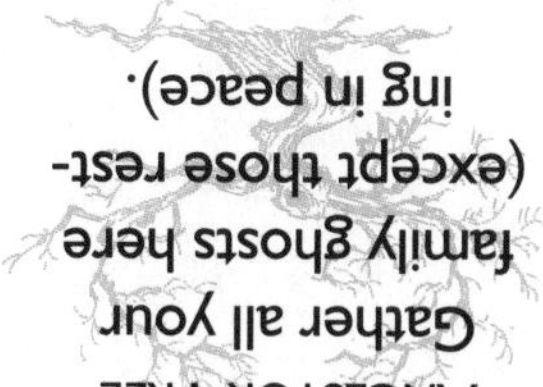

ANCESTOR TREE Gather all your family ghosts here (except those resting in peace).

RIP

FAMILY

RIP

PLOT

Lose way in graveyard. Throw I die. Move back that number of spaces.

Rest in peace. Go directly to RIP.

RIP

Go back to plot. Start again.

Orange **Green**

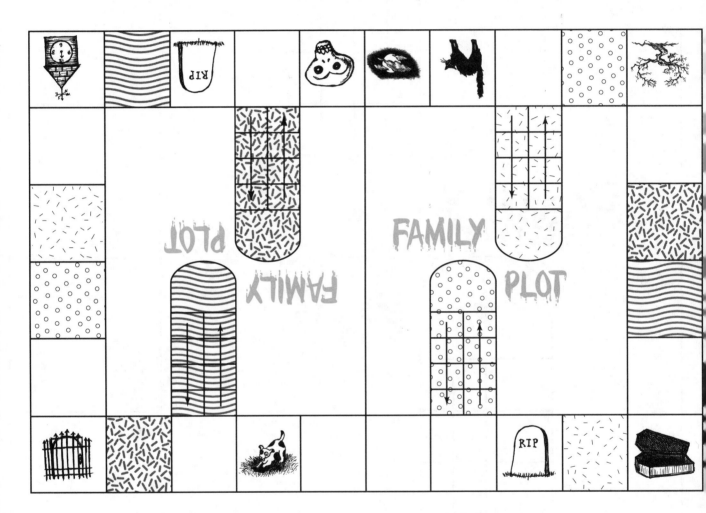

FAMILY PLOT

FAMILY PLOT

Blue **Red**

Gobblin' Grab Game

Don't pass up the chance to grab a treat or two or maybe more! Fun is at the core of this fast-paced game for big groups, so keep the apples moving and you're sure to be a winner.

THIS IS WHAT YOU NEED:

- Gobblin' Grab Greeting pumpkin (on page 41)
- 3 small red apples
- tape player
- musical tape

THIS IS WHAT YOU DO:

1. Have your friends form a circle. Place the Gobblin' Grab pumpkin in the middle of the circle. Give the apples to 3 of the players.

2. One person plays the tape while the other players pass the apples to the left around the circle. When the person stops the music, the players with the apples get to grab a candy from the pumpkin. The last player back in the circle plays the tape for the next round.

3. Repeat Step 2, only pass the apples to the right. Each time the music starts again, the apples are passed in the opposite direction until all the candy is grabbed from the pumpkin.

If you want to know the initial of your true love's name, hold an apple by the stem and twist while saying the alphabet. The letter you say when the apple and stem separate begins the name of your love.

Timely Tales

You don't need to be a fortune-teller to tell a tale with cards. Create new stories using characters and events that change each time the cards are shuffled.

THIS IS WHAT YOU NEED:

- 24 index cards, 3 x 5 inch
- pencil
- paper
- watch with a second hand

THIS IS WHAT YOU DO:

1. Write one word on each index card from the following list:

DRACULA, FRANKENSTEIN, WOLFMAN, WITCH, STRANGER, BOY, OLD WOMAN, GIRL, COUNTRYSIDE, HAUNTED HOUSE, GRAVEYARD, CASTLE, SLINGSHOT, STICK, SHOVEL, ROPE, CAR, MONEY, COMPUTER, JEWELRY, ROBBERY, ATTACK, ACCIDENT, LIES.

2. Shuffle the cards.

RULES:

1. Choose a leader to pick 6 cards and turn them face up on a flat surface.

2. When everyone has had a chance to see the cards, the leader begins timing. Everyone has one minute to think of a tale using as many of the words in the list as possible.

60

3. When time is up, the players tell their tales. The leader keeps score and gives 1 point for each word from the list included and 1 point for the best story.

4. A new leader then reshuffles the cards. The game is repeated until everyone has a chance to be the leader.

5. The player with the most points wins. In case of a tie, the last leader removes Dracula and another card from the stack, scrambles them, and offers them face down to the players. The one who picks Dracula is the winner.

Know someone who doesn't like garlic? He or she could be a vampire. To keep vampires away, hang garlic over your doors and windows, rub it on your chimney and keyholes, and make garlic collars for all your pets.

Pumpkin Patch

Getting tangled in the Pumpkin Patch may seem like a trick, but you'll end up with treats. And when the game is over, you will have a custom-made Halloween sheet for your bed.

THIS IS WHAT YOU NEED:

- newspapers
- twin-size white flat sheet
- permanent markers
- drawing compass or 10-inch plate
- scissors
- 12 small index cards
- small treats

THIS IS WHAT YOU DO:

1. Cover the floor with newspapers to prevent the markers from bleeding through.

2. Draw sixteen 10-inch circles on the sheet. Draw witch's hats in 4 of the circles, pumpkins in 4 others, brooms in 4 more, and candles in the remaining circles. Don't draw the same pictures side by side.

3. Cut the index cards in half. Draw each picture used in the circles 6 times, 1 picture to a card.

RULES:

1. Place the cards face down. Only two people may play during each round. One player turns over a card, then another player touches that picture circle.

2. Each time a card is turned over, the player must touch that new circle while still remaining in contact with the previous circles. The number of circles the player is able to touch before falling will be the number of treats received.

5. Play until everyone gets a chance to be a card-turner and a player.

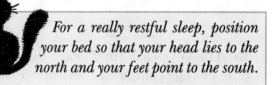

For a really restful sleep, position your bed so that your head lies to the north and your feet point to the south.

61

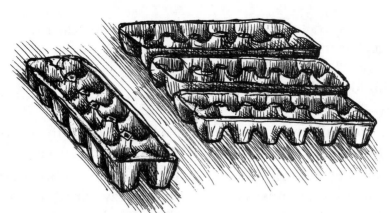

Change Your Luck Game

Start out safe, end up sorry. Your fortune is always changing as your luck turns with each rotation of the game. This is a game for 2, 3, or 4 players. The longer the game goes on, the more *eggs-citing* it gets.

THIS IS WHAT YOU NEED:

- 4 egg cartons, 1-dozen size
- 1 package bean soup mix, containing at least as many different kinds of beans as there are players
- 1 die

THIS IS WHAT YOU DO:

1. Tear the lids off the cartons.
2. Place the cartons side by side.
3. Let each player choose 12 of one kind of bean.

RULES:

1. Each player places their beans in twelve different egg compartments using any or all of the 4 cartons.

2. Players roll the die. The lowest number goes first.

3. Each roll of the die tells the player how many compartments to move. Only 1 bean is moved at a time. The bean is moved in any direction except diagonally—in a straight line or by making left or right turns.

4. If the player lands in a compartment occupied by an opponent, the opponent's bean is taken.

5. When each player has had one turn, one end carton is turned sideways against the others and becomes a safe carton where no bean can be taken, although players may still move their beans into an occupied compartment. After each round, the safe carton is placed last and the new end carton is turned sideways.

6. The player with the last bean or beans left is the winner.

Beans are in many common expressions. To spill the beans means to tell a secret. You don't know beans means the person is ignorant or uneducated.

62

HAUNTED HOUSE CARNIVAL

Which is more fun, a haunted house or a carnival? Now you can have both—the scary atmosphere, creepy creatures, mysterious booths, and frightful food—by making your own Haunted House Carnival.

Planning

A carnival is such a big event, it needs planning. Booths and decorations take time to make. If you are serving food, you need time to shop and cook. Leave about two weeks to put it all together. One person can't do all the work, so get your friends to help—the preparation is half the fun. Count on having at least seven helpers if you do the whole carnival.

Admission

To be admitted to the carnival, each person donates a game, toy, or book. It can be new or used but if used, it must be in good condition. As the donations come in, put them under the Smell-o-pede (on page 50), using one basket for games, one for toys, and one for books. Games are worth five tickets, toys four tickets, and books three tickets. Or tickets may be turned in for candy, one ticket apiece, at the Candy Coffin (page 66).

Ticket Talk

You'll need tickets to give out at the carnival. They may be redeemed for prizes or candy. They're easy to make. Cut six 2-inch strips from the long side of a 9- x 12-inch piece of orange construction paper. From each strip, cut nine 1-inch tickets. Each sheet of construction paper makes 54 tickets. Make at least 2 sheets worth of tickets. You can press Halloween stickers on the tickets to get everyone in the right mood.

Candy Coffin

Lift up the lid and view the candy all laid out for you. Turn in a ticket for each sweet you want to treat yourself to and then pass on the coffin for the next eager eater.

THIS IS WHAT YOU NEED:

- ½ gallon milk or juice carton without plastic cap
- scissors
- ballpoint pen
- 1 brown paper grocery bag
- 3 tufted paper towels
- white glue
- 2 brown or gold pipe cleaners
- assorted candy or granola bars

THIS IS WHAT YOU DO:

1. Wash the carton thoroughly.
2. Completely open the top seam of the carton. Cut down and across the bottom of the spout side. Flip the cut side open to form a coffin lid.
3. Cut open the paper bag. Trace the lid, bottom, and all of the sides of the coffin onto the bag. Cut out the traced pieces. Glue them to the carton and lid, plain side showing.
4. With the pen point, poke 2 holes, about 2 inches apart, in the center of one coffin side. Bend a pipe cleaner in half and twist the halves together. Push the ends into the holes to form a handle for the coffin. Press the ends against the inside. Repeat on the other side.
5. Repeat Step 3 with the paper towels. Glue the towel pieces to the inside of the carton and lid.
6. Pinch the top seam into its original container shape again and tape closed.
7. Fill the coffin with candy bars.

The phrase, "dead as a doornail" has been used for centuries to mean absolutely, certifiably, truly, truly dead. A doornail may refer to the plate, called a nail, behind a door knocker which is struck so often that all life is gone.

66

Fortune-Telling Booth

Look deeply within your crystal ball. See the patterns of fate and time swirling about inside. Concentrate. Then make your predictions about the future.

THIS IS WHAT YOU NEED:

- 2 chairs
- small table
- 6 feet of twine
- clear plastic tape
- scissors
- 3 rolls of crepe paper
- measuring tape
- colored paper
- pen or marker
- newspaper section with horoscope
- glue stick
- glitter
- several see-through scarves
- small fishbowl
- glow-in-the-dark light stick
- Fortune-Teller costume (on page 15)

THIS IS WHAT YOU DO:

1. Put the chairs and table in a corner of the room. Stretch the twine as high up as you can reach, from one wall to the other, in front of the table and chairs. Tape each end of the twine securely. Cut 5-foot lengths of crepe paper, enough to make a curtain. Fold one end over the twine and tape in place.

2. Cut the colored paper into star shapes. Write a fortune on each star. Look at newspaper horoscopes for inspiration. Make about 30 to 50 stars, depending on the size of the carnival.

3. Turn the stars over. Rub the glue stick on the back of each star. Sprinkle with glitter.

4. Place the scarves loosely into the fishbowl. Put the light stick in the middle of the scarves. Don't pack the scarves too tightly or the light won't shine through. Turn the fishbowl upside down on the table to form a crystal ball.

5. Put on the Fortune-Teller costume. Seat a person opposite you. Have the person ask a question as you both concentrate on the crystal ball.

6. Run your hands gently over the crystal ball. Give a positive but vague answer. For example, if you are asked, "Will I go to camp this summer?" answer something like, "I see you swimming in cool water." Maybe it's at camp, maybe not—it's up to the person to figure that out.

7. Send the person away with a star fortune, a prediction for him or her alone.

> *Astrology is a form of predicting the future by studying the positions of heavenly bodies and their effects on humans.*

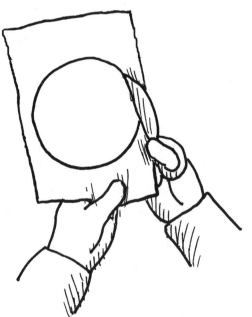

Jack-o'-Lantern Toss

This is a beanbag toss game. It requires a little sewing, but sew what? You can do it. Look on page 24 for how to make the running stitch.

THIS IS WHAT YOU NEED:

- 3 orange felt squares (available in fabric stores)
- pencil
- scissors
- needle
- orange thread
- 1 black felt square
- glue
- 16-ounce bag of dried peas or small dried beans
- large carton
- thick black marker
- table
- tickets

THIS IS WHAT YOU DO:

1. A day or so before the carnival, prepare the beanbags. Fold 1 orange square in half. In pencil, draw a circle on one side. Cut out the circle through both layers of felt.

2. Cut out jack-o'-lantern eyes, nose, and mouth from the black felt. Glue onto one side of the orange felt.

3. Place the two circles together and, using a running stitch, sew around the circle,

½ inch from the edge. Leave about 1 inch open to form a pocket.

4. Fill the pocket with peas or beans. Finish sewing it closed to make a beanbag. Repeat Steps 1 through 4 with the other orange squares.

5. On the carton, draw a large circle with the marker. Cut out jack-o'-lantern eyes, nose, and mouth large enough for a beanbag to go through. Outline the face parts in black. Draw curved, vertical lines to make the circle look like a pumpkin.

RULES:

1. Place the table against a wall. Put the carton on the table.

2. Have each player take 3 giant steps backward. The player tosses the bean-bags at the pumpkin. Give 1 ticket for each beanbag that goes into one of the openings.

THE PORTRAIT OF DORY AND RAY

Carlo stared at the painting of Great-great-aunt Dory. Something was strange about it. Ray, the black cat that sat on her lap, was missing. How could part of a painting disappear?

Everyone said Aunt Dory was a witch, but Carlo needed proof before he would believe it.

Carlo felt something furry dash across his feet. He looked down and saw paw prints on the carpet. His socks were covered with black hairs. He followed the prints down the hall. They led to the door and stopped. Now he heard scratching on the other side, but when he opened the door, nothing was there. What is going on? thought Carlo.

He felt a cold chill run up his spine and suddenly he knew it could be true. As he ran back through the hall, he thought he heard someone whisper, "Ray. Where are you, Ray?" When he looked up at the painting, he had his proof. . . .

Mummy Knows Your Birthday Booth

The mummy has lived for centuries and unwrapped the mysteries of the universe. It knows everything—including your birthday! Talk with your mummy and connect with the ages.

THIS IS WHAT YOU NEED:

- 6 same-size cartons, at least 20 inches wide
- 8 heavy books
- packing or masking tape, about 2 inches wide
- thick black marker
- white, twin-size flat sheet
- Ancient Mummy costume (on page 13)
- 2 chairs
- assistant
- tickets

THIS IS WHAT YOU DO:

1. Make the columns a few days before. Remove any sharp staples from the cartons. If the cartons have loose flaps, tuck them inside.

2. Place 1 carton short-end up. Put 4 heavy books at the bottom. This is the base of a column for the mummy's tomb. Then place 2 more cartons, short-end up, on top of the base. Tape each carton securely to the one below it to form a column. Make a second column with the other 3 cartons.

3. With the marker, draw a stone pattern on the columns. Color in some of the stones, but not all.

4. On the day of the carnival, place the columns about 4½ feet apart. Gather one corner of the sheet. Tape it to the top of one of the columns. Extend the sheet to the other column and tape it.

5. Put on the mummy costume. Sit in one of the chairs behind the sheet. Have your assistant draw aside the sheet to admit a player, who then sits in the other chair.

6. The mummy asks 5 questions, such as, "Was it cold when you were born?" or "Do you have two numbers in the day of your birthday?" After the questions are asked, the mummy must guess either the day or the month of the player's birthday. If the mummy guesses wrong, the player gets a ticket. If the mummy guesses correctly, the mummy and the assistant sing the "Happy Birthday" song, but no ticket is given.

Q. Why was the mummy laid to rest?

A. Because he was tired.

71

Tombstone Rubbings Booth

Create your own graveyard with UDOs: unidentified dying objects. There are no names on these tombstones, but they look like the real thing.

THIS IS WHAT YOU NEED:

- sharpened pencils
- white unlined paper
- scissors
- magazines with Halloween pictures (optional)
- poster board, any color, 22 x 28 inches
- white glue
- stick-on letters
- 2 large plastic trash bags with built-in ties
- 4 folding chairs
- table
- plastic trays with a raised design
- crayons or colored chalk
- black or gray construction paper

THIS IS WHAT YOU DO:

1. Ahead of time, draw on paper or cut from a magazine 6 small pictures (under 4 inches) of bats, witches, monsters, pumpkins, or any Halloween related subject.

2. Cut the poster board into six 8- x 11-inch pieces, leaving a 4-inch strip. Glue the pictures onto the strip. Cut out around the outline of each pictured shape. In the center of each 8- x 11-inch piece of poster board, glue one of the cut-out pictures to create a raised surface.

3. Using the stick-on letters, stick one of these epitaphs under each of the pictures:

REST IN PEACE	I'M GONE
HERE I LIE	FORGET ME NOT
RIP	GOOD-BYE

4. On the day of the carnival, cut open the trash bags along one seam and the bottom. Snip the tie in the top grooves. Pull out the tie from the ends.

5. Now, set up your booth. Make a 4-foot square with the chairs, seats facing inward. Stand behind 2 of the chairs. Stretch out one bag. Overlap it on the tops of the chair backs and tie it down, to form a graveyard wall. Repeat with the other chairs. Set up the table between the chairs with these items: trays, pictures with epitaphs, pencils, crayons, chalk, white paper, colored paper, and scissors.

6. Have each person make a rubbing. First, choose a background tray pattern, place a piece of white paper on top, and rub over the paper with the side of a pencil, crayon, or chalk. Next, center the same paper on one of the pictures and rub over the picture and epitaph.

7. Round off the top edges of the paper for a tombstone shape. Glue the tombstone to a piece of construction paper.

Q. Why was Skeleton's book a bestseller?

A. Because it had a good plot.

73

Wart the Witch's Nose Game

Every witch knows she needs a wart. Help her get one with this easy-to-make wall game. The winner gets a *re-wart*.

THIS IS WHAT YOU NEED:

- pencil
- poster board, 22 x 28 inches
- marker
- poster putty
- blindfold
- tickets

THIS IS WHAT YOU DO:

1. Ahead of time, draw a witch's face and hat on the poster board with the pencil. Then go over the drawing with the marker.

2. On the day of the carnival, put a blob of putty on each back corner of the poster board. Press the poster board to the wall.

RULES:

1. Have the player stand 6 feet from the witch. Give the player a dime-size putty wart.

2. Blindfold and turn the player around 3 times. Point the player toward the witch.

3. The player walks toward the witch and presses the wart where the nose might be. If the wart lands anywhere on the witch's face, the player wins one ticket. If it lands on the nose, the player gets a ticket and another turn.

Superstition says that because of their own wartlike skin, toads cause warts on anyone who touches them.

Eerie Eating Center

Working up an appetite at the Haunted House Carnival? No ordinary treat will satisfy that monster hunger and thirst. Here is the most unusual food west of Transylvania. You'll find the recipes starting on page 31.

THIS IS WHAT YOU NEED:

- marker
- orange construction paper
- 1 large or 2 small tables
- tablecloths (optional)
- transparent tape
- paper plates
- cups
- napkins
- serving utensils

THIS IS WHAT YOU DO:

1. With the marker, write out the menu on a sheet of construction paper:

   WIGGLY WORM SANDWICH WITH DEVIL'S SALSA . . . 3 TICKETS

   KNOCKOUT VAMPIRE PUNCH . . . 1 TICKET

   and so forth.

2. Decorate the wall where you'll be setting up the table or tables. For decorating tips, see the chapter on Devilish Decorating (page 41).

3. Place the table near the wall, leaving a space for the server. Cover the table with the cloth if you're using one. Tape the menu to the wall or table. Put out the plates, cups, napkins, and utensils.

4. Set out the food and punch. The server will take tickets and give out the food.

Q. What did the troll get when he bumped into the apple tree?

A. Applesores

A VAMPIRE BAT

A vampire bat named Dwight
was puzzled one Halloween night.
When he said, "Trick or treat,"
people ran down the street;
all he wanted was one little bite!

GHASTLY RIDDLES

Q. **Who wears a cape, has fangs, and says quack, quack, quack?**

A. Count Duckula

Q. **Where does Dracula keep his savings?**

A. In the blood bank

Q. **What witch helps to pack your groceries?**

A. The brown paper bag

Q. **What candy does a snake give out for Halloween?**

A. Chocolate hisses

Q. **What's green, mean, and super clean?**

A. A witch who flew through a car wash

Q. How does a witch keep her haunted house cool?

A. She puts on the scare conditioner

Q. What did the ghost receive when he won first place at the fair?

A. A boo ribbon

Q. What did the ghost receive for last place in the haunting contest?

A. The boo-by prize

Q. What happened when one witch moved in with the other witch?

A. They became broom mates

BOOOOOO!